Musandam moons

Musandam moons

SELECTED POEMS AND SONGS

Ed Fram

F E FRAM

MUSANDAM MOONS

My delicate dreams drift
On midnight's Musandam moons
And evening's stiff tiff
Has passed too soon ...

So play me that music, my Musandam muse
Lead me to the eternal King of Ormus
Singing still, in the Sea of Fars
Singing still, no matter where you are

And rouse me from my slothful slumber
Drag me bleary-eyed and under
But keep closed the eyes of the unknowing
And together we'll keep going
With my ears filled to the brim
Carried on your Hormuzian harp hymns

When all you've read leads to a Godhead
you always fled
When the last tears have all been shed
Bled dry to see the children protected and well-fed
"Then you'll be a man my boy!" father always said
With that in mind, I now thee wed
Until we be dead
Until we be dead ...

Wishing for health and wealth but getting malady and hunger instead
Dreaming of better times laying here in bed
And painting the sky all the earth's colours; except red
For red is the rose of regret you once said
Yes, red is for the rose of regret ...

The sun supervises the super-drying of the damned

Wild flowers still hold meaning for the land
Needing each other like a bolt needs its thunder
The squally rains are blowing us under
So take these roses of regret
Take them from me so I can forget
That tomorrow's a day we'll never get
Yes, tomorrow's a day we'll never get …

Like the tear I gave you, don't you recall?
I loved too easily, my true downfall
Some want sweet, some seek long-haul
Some are made to fall on the sword like Saul

A tear filled with grief, too heavy to fall
I drag this load like a laden lead ball
Two bodies, one coffin to the resting hall
In time with the bells of Saint Paul

A tear yet felt and formed to fall
Look out, it'll come like a tidal wall!
To wash away one and all
Separating vacant voices from His call

A tear so silent says it all
The wailing wind, this black shawl
Whispers of hope in ears so small
Giants cut down, on their knees they crawl

A tear to give life, like the rain that falls
Black is but a colour – that's all
The sunken ship will make landfall
In time with the bells of Saint Paul

Yet here we are again
Where twisted tales pass for news

Transfixed but bemused
With the social stains of the lonely
There's beauty in pain
So says Leonard Cohen
Between cries of Stella I'm bleeding

Yesteryear's snow, in rivers it flows
Changed but not forgotten
But when tomorrow's winds blow
Will it be back, clean as cotton?

I love you still
I'll love you until
I love you only
By then you'll see
It's only me
That you're needing

The flower asks not the reason
As the sun sets the season
There's beauty in confusion
Like ancient souls in modern times
We fill our minds
With ideas that need feeding

See yesteryear's snow, in rivers how it flows
Changed but not forgotten
But when tomorrow's winds blow
Will it be back as clean as cotton?

Our time again, it may seem
To go on chasing silver dreams
Downstream
Where love, from our eyes was stole
Oh, how full of fleeting glances!

Now a surfeit of sorrow, to swallow us whole
Retracing steps of first dances

Tears don't know which way to go
My heart beats just for show
So many ways to say I tried
Only ever one goodbye
A sweet note for reference
"The change made no difference"
Pain came and it'll go
Leaving me human

But how many days pass between
each sunrise, seen through your eyes?
With tortured tangles of a man
Making funny angles as only you can
Out of the straightest of lines
And as the death rod strikes its chime
Then you'll know how hard it is to turn on a light
in the dark

Bouncing shadows across broken bars
Full winter moons come in jaded jars
So tired of the cold they're in
What's left is sold, so I'd better get going
Leaving only memories in the mirror
Of all those nameless faces
and faceless names
That time won't remember

And now, so clearly I hear the wide-eyed sailor
He's telling of a beauty not yet known
Listen! As he speaks so softly
of elements pure, but never shown
He tells of drowning in the waters

that protect and defend us
When the waves have lost their charm
When our fortress has formed against us
Bringing danger to mourning mothers
and daggers from the house of harm
Now tell me what do you really see,
the same affection or just some kind of apathy?

Hear the warble of the warrior
He's calling the tribes to arms
As we drift away silently
Sailing on seas so calm
A tear for every occasion
Beyond the house of harm

Bitterness and tragedy, I found plenty of it with you
Solace in solitude and the meaning of existence too
And life's empty promises
Somehow they're leaving me fulfilled
If we can't go with the flow
Tell me who else will?
But who would bet against you,
holding all the aces as you do?
You made me the accomplice
The crime was finding love in you
Others nonchalant and novice
You left them without a clue
Ripped both asunder, no promise
While I found my love in you

I hear the warble of the warrior
He's calling the tribes to arms
As we drift away silently
Sailing on seas so calm
A tear for every occasion

Beyond the house of harm

The crazy, creative type, he's left all alone
With a kiss so warm and gentle
Imagination must claim him as his own
As the three ravens return to climes oriental
From whence they've once flown
But this night, it belongs to us at last
So take the red rope, reel us in to shore
The laughter must die down
The clown will cry some more
And the sails will soon slacken
Promise you'll never let go!
The skies will surely blacken
"I promise I'll never let go!"
There's nothing natural about nature
Only a game of cat and mouse
The reaper's always out to get you
Only harm comes from his house

Hear the warble of the warrior
He's calling the tribes to arms
As we drift away silently
Sailing on seas so calm
A tear for every occasion
Beyond the house of harm

But where were you when I needed you most?
Hopes hammered to the ground
I'm not dead yet, though I've seen my ghost
The final cannonball blew without a sound
They say life is but a memory
I'm trying so hard to forget
A friend's foe is my enemy
You can't turn a page without regret

But I can't forget your smile, no not yet
I can't forget your smile, no not yet
And who but the hungry have tasted it all?
Who but the sinner knows of mercy divine?
Autumn-scented leaves decay before a fall
Even a fool must be right some of the time

Fools like us!
Before nothingness came to mean everything to us
They were there
The sky's eyes peaking out from beneath their blanket of black
Daringly, like a callow creature unready for the stillness of slumber
I thought we had forever
Then nothingness came to mean everything to us
But our light is there too
Shining for those yet born
Still seeking eternity
Still looking for a cradle to call home …

Like a song in space
Or a dance in the dark
What use a car to race
with no place to park?
As slogans shout out
"Death to capitalism!"
A post-romantic collectivism
With corporates on a cross
And the poet at a loss
playing with words
For sentences never served
his time well
Better the drunkard
watched as he fell
More sorrows than solutions
But they wish him well

Always knowing life will see The Thinker
Cut down to size
You can see it in his laughless eyes
Written out of history
In pencil

A southerly swinging in the trees
The rich do as they please
Never pausing to ponder
Lest they take leave of living
The wronged forced into forgiving
The abandoned still seeking their King
Captive to the capricious
With their unrelenting streams of hate
But they'll cease to flow before the date
Where scarlet girls are known to wait
Like dusts of desire in the air
For those going here and those going nowhere

But this boy never cared what he read
Even less to him what was said
Sensing that between the lines
We're all dancing on dimes
So work the wounds
The words will follow
Lie softly, lie softly
Every man's grave is hollow
Yes, every man's grave is hollow

Like that emptiness filling the void between the unboxed ideas and
dreams of others
Siren cries of a child so sickeningly salubrious
A worldview that never sees God as anything more than an inconve-
nience, so dubious
Amidst tatty black and white photos

(Never in that order, except linguistically)
There's all the colour in the world now
But some things don't change

Some are born to run
Others dying to live
Some just want fun
Others just want to know how much you can give
"But sometimes the truth obstructs the Truth"
So sayeth the sayer of sooth
A weaker seeker must find for himself
That all the riches aren't much wealth

Some care only if they're feeding
Some'll ask you what you're reading
No one will come when you're bleeding
Life spilled like milk
Never to be cried for
With perfect pins
To nail you down
That's what you'd die for
But sorrow drowned the spring buds
In its watery wails
So, calmly on she sails
Calmly on she sails

Who to have in your bed, who to wed
A lifestyle magazine choice,
like Damascus tiles or veneer vials
For me, laying on this broken bed
Of undreamt dreams
Can't say what was said
But I'll tell you what it means
If only you'd come and join me
Collecting words in a closet

Full to bursting!
Take away the brush
The painter's drawing conclusions
Unfit for mass consumption

We're all consumed by consumption
Contrived to deprive all but the one percent
I see you're occupying a different space now
But you're still the same gal, only on the ascent
So worried you haven't got nearly enough
But you don't have to think about sleeping rough
Green eyes see the world differently
There's no black and white,
only shadows of time, in time you'll see

When the shoes don't fit like they should
The tears have nowhere to fall, like they could
The earth is dry where you once stood
Sentenced to read every word
But understanding not one
Haven't you heard
you aren't the one?
Free to enslave
But enslaved by your freedom!
Playing for time
But time's been kicked to touch!
So you'd better walk the line
And quit expecting so much
Yes, quit expecting so much!
You're screaming blue, a colour I once knew too
But I've never known a lung more likely to falter
Beyond here lie layers of life anew
with the sacred scarified at the alter

There's no range too strange

Neon or nylon; man-made meditations
Machinations of an unmaintained mind
But there's no use looking at the attendant
Ask the ghoul of Giza
He'll tell you the price of a quart of gas
To quench the thirst of your Roller, so resplendent
Here where the clouds reign
And the homesick are awake, dependent
On sharp comforts of pain
You can find plenty of parking ...

Amid the washed-up crab-covered carcass
Bagged and tagged: "Death by dangerous company"
Wild winds with hell's flames to harness
Carry letters from a father that aren't for me ...

If we hadn't quite cross paths
You could almost have called it fate
In love at the same time
But on different dates
Go! Open each door
We've got nothing to hide
There's nothing in the cellar
Not a thing inside
Save for rats and river water
And sailors' dreams of better tides

Where does the rain go
When it's tired of being teary-eyed?
Does the river still chase the sea
When all its waters have dried?

There still, the washed-up crab-covered carcass
"Death by dangerous company"
Wild winds with hell's flames to harness

Carry letters from a father that aren't for me ...

There's one for her bravery
One ending slavery
One within a day
One without pay
One for all to read
One admonishing greed
One for the fountain new
One making many from few
But where's the one you're needing?

One for her hunger
One in silence yonder
One to never fear
One holding all dear
One to drink the cup
One to pull us up
One to lead the way
One holds still as the branches sway
But where is the one you're needing?

One sent with the lightest touch
One is for keeping watch
One made for those that suffer slow
One gives without a show
One for faithful fortitude
One embracing sacred solitude
One for forgiving
One to help those dying for a living
But where's the one you're needing?

Now the reaper's in range,
no time for goodbye
Not a thing I'd change,

now that's a lie!
But isn't it strange
to forgive without asking why?

So play me that music, my Musandam muse
Lead me to the eternal King of Ormus
Singing still, in the Sea of Fars
Singing still, no matter where you are

For my delicate dreams drift
On midnight's Musandam moons
And evening's stiff tiff
Has passed too soon ...

© Ed Fram 2018

Lady Luck

The hummingbirds are grounded
The harp, a statue of silent strings
Take the diamond you were handed
Place it with all the other useless things
Lady Luck has spoken
The clover has lost a leaf
You thought they were joking
When they said death is no relief

The ship's been brought home to harbour,
engulfed by the seas she sailed
Your pedestal's fit for a maharaja,
adored for your successes,
not the successive times you failed
But Lady Luck has spoken
The clover has lost another leaf
Your prayers were just a token
To hide from your true belief

At the border line we did part
As the bell's tongue clapped out another chime
In time with the beat of your heart
To tell you it's closing time
For Lady Luck has spoken
The clover has lost another leaf
Now there's no use in hoping
That your time here will be brief

The choir has sung its sorrowful song
Tomorrow has buried the past
It's all out of sight, but not really gone
The wind has blown its last
And Lady Luck has spoken

The clover has lost all its leaves
The fortune teller has woken
And a robe for your child she weaves
Yes, a robe for your child she weaves ...

© Ed Fram 2021

Been and gone

I'll be leaving with the stars, blown out like candles
The same breath that'll take me to seas afar
Leave your flowers by my gate, the hour is getting late
And there's no telling where we are …

From the harbour sands to someplace upland,
thick with bees a-hummin'
We'd prepared for rain,
climbing the fuchsia-lined lane
As the angels with their harps came a-strummin'

The mist on the hill seems so far until,
you're close enough to breathe it
Like the love I had for you sailing in the blue,
when you just wouldn't believe it

Your shadow in the tide gets longer
As I ride by each sinking sun
So far and wide like the world's hunger
To chase what's already been and gone
Yes, to chase what's already been and gone …

© Ed Fram 2021

From London to Duluth

Lord knows who crowned you,
the Queen of my heart!
Were you lost when I found you,
puzzling over Picasso's art?
Your mystical manner turned my world upside down, like luckless Job's
You tore down my crown and accused me of being in robbed robes

It's been a minute before midnight for a long old while
And I hear falling in love is going out of style
We danced naked, bare beneath the truth
Knowing we'd make it anywhere, from London to Duluth …

You came in on steely seas, the weary traveller here to please
In danger I'd been a dabbler, never lived a moment I didn't seize
But I must confess a little shiver came down me, it came down from my
face to my feet
When I saw a slither of your leg, from underneath your neat pleat

It's been a minute before midnight for a long old while
And I hear falling in love is going out of style
We danced naked, bare beneath the truth
Knowing we'd make it anywhere, from London to Duluth …

"Don't be bereft" you said, as you turned to wave at my door
I realised then you'd never left, we'd been here before
With our jail bars overlapping, in adjoining cells
When the inspector comes tapping, cast him under your spell

It's been a minute before midnight for a long old while
And I hear falling in love is going out of style
We danced naked, bare beneath the truth
Knowing we'd make it anywhere, from London to Duluth …

That kind of beauty

You can crown your dome with a parasol
Drape your neck with the jewels you stole
But your purpose drifts so distantly, like a port lost at sea
Tell me, how much pain must there be, to contain that kind of beauty?

With no place to hide, tethered to each tide
And nothing but a broken temple inside, in which to confide
How could you ever be free?
Now tell me, is it him you see while you're here looking at me?

You always were a few steps ahead of anything I ever said
All has been settled and seen, but who bled the roses red?
Take my dreams, put them with yours
And tell me, does it leave you wanting more - will it open heaven's doors?

You can crown your dome with a parasol
Drape your neck with the jewels you stole
But your purpose drifts so distantly, like a port lost at sea
Tell me, how much pain must there be, to contain that kind of beauty?

© Ed Fram 2021

Nothing left to lose

The lion loves tenderly, only that which rules his heart
Men of ancient hands slowly build temples in the sand,
so their souls may swiftly depart
The love I give affectionately, I give full from the start
There's nothing left to lose, when nothing is left lost
So play the hand and don't count the cost

You begged me "please oh please!", to take you in
But I was never really into that kinda thing
Like the fair breeze, the fruits in trees are chasin'
But you didn't know where it would end or even how to begin
Now who'll explain why they lay slain by a hurricane for the tasting?

Only the painter knows which came first, the rainbow or the ark
When all is vanishing before us now
Do you dare a kiss before it gets dark?
I heard the answer and you knew it too somehow
There's nothing left to lose, when nothing is left lost
So play the hand and don't count the cost

© Ed Fram 2021

The sincerity of heaven

Use the words the Word has given
Not those taught from men's tongues unleavened
Use the words the Word has given
Not those brought out without the sincerity of heaven

Let the light spill out from the Light
To touch the gloom inside us
Let the light spill out from the Light
To feel your presence beside us

Lead the way to the Way
When the roads divide and conquer
Lead the way to the Way
Cleanse me to "not guilt your honour"

Speak to the son from the Son
Truthful whispers from the breeze
Speak to this son from the Son
Hear their nightly calls and pleas

And I'll use the words the Word has given
Not those taught from men's tongues unleavened
I'll use the words the Word has given
Not those brought out without the sincerity of heaven

© Ed Fram 2021

Midnight in Sicily

A lover sings for her king
For whom, she's readied a dominion
Of matching jumpers and matching opinions
The orchid keeper sleeps, he knows his role
As the bees bring food for the soul
and philosophies to live by
It's why we write, it's why we sing
It's why the lover sings for her king

The stepping stone to nowhere, you must leave it out
Money don't talk, it shouts
So trust your gut and mind the company that you keep
We're not dead yet and the climb is steep
So let tomorrow worry about the future
For we have today, yes we have today

A lover speaks freely to her king
No mention of the children, their names you shan't bring
For the understudy says we'll meet again
But the careless people and plots of the wise
are there to tell us otherwise
Now why does the beauty carry a frisky frock
To leave the uninitiated a bolt, a shock?
With her promises of hidden interiors
Unshackled from the condor and her superiors
To look behind their masks and see
they're sleeping with the dogs

Across the ocean and the sea's great houses
Rests the cold heat of dead embers and silent spouses
But one day as a tiger roaring she'll return
To see there's nothing left to envy
She was a queen in the desert

A reed unshaken by the winds between river and sea
Among past shanasheel and the present clutter, there she lay, there she lay
Nothing seems to matter, not anymore
there's nothing left to say
It's all beyond the belief of unbelievers anyway

Yet the wondering one is still not accounted for
Is it him stepping naked into the novel bookstore?
Three dozen and four score more!
Three dozen and four score more!
He'll try to sell you anything
In the shepherd's life nothing's sure
Meanwhile it's midnight in Sicily

Even the ravaged tree may live on as paper
But what will come of us when our leaves are soil-clad and ashen?
"Spend a third to save a quarter, then you too can cash in!"
On a daughter that brought her and me
Out of a wilderness now long past
Out of a wilderness now long past
Before the rebellion inside reveals at last
What we all have known since the beginning
Meanwhile day breaks in our hearts
And it's midnight in Sicily

Scarlet

Unmade man, made unmanly
By what he longs to be
With unfed mind, he hungers
For words, his only bread
Alone he often wanders
Till his feet bled red
Till his feet bled red ...
The truth is fixed on broken promises
Every -ism pored over by every -ist
But what shall remain, beyond the morning mist?

Unmade man, made unmanly
By what he now calls free
Pitying the shadow
Chained to dark as day
He goes across the mountain meadow
And along the wagon way
And along the wagon way ...
The truth is fixed on broken promises
Every -ism pored over by every -ist
But what shall remain, beyond the midday mist?

Unmade man, made unmanly
By what he used to be
Now each day bringing more decay
But her scarlet scarf's still weakly waving
Though there's nothing left to say
With no more left for saving
With no more left for saving ...
The truth is fixed on broken promises

Every -ism pored over by every -ist
Nothing shall remain, beyond the midnight mist ...

© Ed Fram 2016

Seeking a song

When falling back with no place to land
Beware those who offer to lend a hand
For they'll run off with all your money
Ignore the buzz, they'll never give you any honey
No use complaining to those thinking it's funny
They'll say walk it off, to see you stride hither and yon

But surely you will tell me what's going on
For you were gone all night long
Are you looking for a place to belong?
Like unsung words seeking a song
Are we not two rights undoing a wrong?
Oh please tell me, what's going on …

There's no turning back if you choose to stumble across
Theirs ain't a bridge you'd wanna double-cross
Salute their hero, though his medals have lost their gloss
There's no use for servants, without a master to wait upon
But when you ask him if it's good, he'll say it's bon!

So will you tell me what's going on?
Again, you were gone all night long
Are you looking for a place to belong?
Like unsung words seeking a song
Are we not two rights undoing a wrong?
Oh please tell me, what's going on …

Ask the poet at the stairs of the Sorbonne
Where lovers meet to trade kisses and cares
To agree what's scarcely sacred and what's rightly theirs
On the fronts of the free and tails of the debonair
A place to solemnly declare
"All that breathes will have no breath left!"

For the misery to come will leave all bereft
Why can't you see, we're just too far gone?

So that's all you'll tell of what's going on
Of where you went all night long?
Are you still seeking a place to belong?
Like unsung words searching for a song
Are we not two rights undoing a wrong?
Please tell me more of what's going on …

Though cast'd of water, we'll form not tears
To be rounded and routed with sharpened spears
From those in the shadows now seen clear
Above the wailing walls, they'll heed no call
A final fall, a soot'd chain and ball
All to be seen, where the light once shone

But tell me plain, what's going on
Let me know, it's been hidden too long!
Are you still seeking a place to belong?
Like unsung words searching for a song
Are we no more two rights undoing a wrong?
Tell me anything my dear, just not so long …

A song for Billy

Billy says "Get the coffins crowned
Before the sun comes down
It's time to take 'em underground!"
They're tightening the noose
To loosen the tongue
But dead men don't talk
Before the bell's been rung

There ain't no use living yesterday on a loop
But tomorrow ain't the time to feel good
You shoulda done it while you could
For this ain't the place to lose your mind
The headroom for that, you just can't find
All the space is filled by charcoal lilies
And fast-shooting, slow-talking mates of Billy's …

Billy says she got a short skirt 'n' tall demands
A flick of the wrist, anything she commands
But she's scared where all her possessions might end
So she'll ask that you be her friend
Yet her feelings, she keeps them well hid
She knows these gems can't be parted with

There ain't no use living yesterday on a loop
But tomorrow ain't the time to feel good
You shoulda done it while you could
For this ain't the place to lose your mind
The headroom for that, you just can't find
All the space is filled by charcoal lilies
And fast-shooting, slow-talking mates of Billy's …

Billy thinks some be looking for their fame
Some wanna be known by a new name

Some be seeking the finest gold
Some wanna be left alone in the cold
Like Selene watching over her queens of the night
But the phone exchange ain't swapping messages, only light
So I'll watch 'em go to and fro, moonrise to sunset
The conquerors of early Saxon kings and lasting regret

There ain't no use living yesterday on a loop
But tomorrow ain't the time to feel good
You shoulda done it while you could
For this ain't the place to lose your mind
The headroom for that, you just can't find
All the space is filled by charcoal lilies
And fast-shooting, slow-talking mates of Billy's ...

© Ed Fram 2016

Troubadour's tune

I'll ready the tune, but choose silence and signs
When the words just won't come to you
It's better than singing careless rhymes
To those listening, searching for a clue
But when the meaning has gone from your chimes
They'll still look to you
Yes, they'll still look to you ...

What you're hearing now,
Whispers from the ceiling
They'll always follow you somehow
It's all you'll ever be leaving
that and this scarf you're weaving
For a poet's unborn son
Who's crying, why am I the only one?
When the door shuts to his darkened room
Where the scent of suffering's in bloom
And for him, father's tune can't come too soon ...
He's already looking to you
Yes, he's already looking to you ...

Wistful words carried on streams of dream dust
Are now speaking of tea at high noon
You've seen them before, they're vapours you trust
It'll surely be enough to fill their waning moons
Them that are fixing their eyes skyward
And whose ears are pricked forward
To whom this tune can't come too soon
But meaning has vanished from your hand
Will my ghosts ever play host?

Or will they still look to you?
Will your love always hold your hand by this coast?
And will she still look to you too?

The sea of night

They say too much thought will kill you
But not enough will make you frown
A distraction can be the main attraction too
Now tell me, in tears will death not drown?

Release me from these cash cuffs
I'll burns them paper chains
He'll know everyone's had enough
When there's no one on his train

I'll turn to stars bathing in the sea of night
As the sun salutes the moon
I can't forget you my love, try though I might
Your scent still fills our room

He tries so hard to be like them
But those hands betray his working roots
He ain't got a chance with them
No matter how fast his best gun shoots

I wait patiently at the door
Feeling for your breath
You don't come home no more
Can tears drown death?

They say too much thought will kill you
But not enough will make you frown
A distraction can be the main attraction too
Now tell me, in tears will death not drown?

© Ed Fram 2017

Columbia calling

The top girls are eating Chaos, uplifting their existence
Amid architecture's near-death experience
of Marian masterworks
Meanwhile it's autumn in Europe
And I'm chasing embers to the gates of sorrow, where Capitalism lurks
Like a ghost that's never paid for
And the stars, how they shimmer in the moonshine, always wanting more!
But honey you're still looking fine, just don't forget to close the door

Lacy and Lilly are taking their sauna on tour
There's no appetite for new ideas at the slaughterhouse
They're trying to leave the kids something secure
This ain't no time to start feeding the lion to the mouse
For each man carries the law in the palm of his hand
You don't need a map to know the lay of the land
And the stars, o how they shimmer in the moonshine, always wanting
more!
Honey you're still looking fine, just pick yourself up from off the floor

The hackers say it's Columbia calling
Their backers know it's not yet morning
In the handwritten hamlets of no fixed abode
In the naked palaces, so white it looks like it snowed
Where the King invites you to try anything from his threadbare wardrobe
As long as it doesn't interfere with the stars
Just look how they shimmer in the moonshine, always wanting more!
Honey you're still looking fine, if only you seemed more sure ...

Leaving Rose

Her hair hangs long
Short is the skirt
I know looking's wrong
But who you calling a flirt?
Go ahead, unmake your bed
But leave them roses behind
I'm just another fool you said
And you ain't the loving kind

The same plaque's back
It's searching for a cause
There's no plan of attack
Paper tigers without claws
Go ahead, unmake your bed
But leave them roses behind
I'm just another fool you said
And you ain't the loving kind

With hate dressed as love
It don't fit so good
And you write "see above"
Cos you think you should
So go ahead, unmake your bed
But leave them roses behind
I'm just another fool you said
And you ain't the loving kind

The Earl of Oxford Street

To him she's everything
Brick on brick rose her frame
Her fame's all in his name
He's in debt to the world, but he owes it nothing
Twirling buck chips just to feel something
Now the Earl knows rubbing pennies won't keep him warm
But staring at her will, the same face just a different form
To him she's everything still ...

"Move on, move on!"
"The Queen of Time has not yet sung!"
No use, his top hat's on the bottom rung
It's aside the super's desk
For the Earl, just part of life's cruel test
For drowning girls in priceless pearls
From the deepest ocean bed
Where his heart now lies
Wishing it had listened to her voice instead
She's here again now, with a love only seen in a mother's eyes
For mile-a-minute Harry, rushed off his feet
He's being mistaken as the Vagabond of Bond Street
"There's no use for you now, there's no one left for you to greet."
But the Showman of Shopping still has his maker to meet
So say a prayer for the Earl of Oxford Street ...

To him she's everything
Brick on brick rose her frame
Her fame's all in his name
He's in debt to the world, but he owes it nothing
Twirling buck chips just to feel something

Now the Earl knows rubbing pennies won't keep him warm
But staring at her will, the same face just a different form
To him she's everything still ...

Crazy farm cares

I made my peace with death
But mourn my own demise
Nothing but memories left
Forever fading, but the sun will rise ...

Like a gentleman's need for tweed
To separate him from the masses
Misunderstanding all you read
Chewing on spat out molasses
A delirium of its own making, there's no need to sound the alarm
A fear in them that you're faking, now which way to the crazy farm?

You don't give kisses light
They come only after dark
You think they're worth more to the blind than sight
But all I need is a gentle word or a kind remark

Take care not to be in too much of a hurry
Before you know it, life'll rush right by you
Ah! How for each coin we run and scurry
But you better bury it before it buries you

Never walk beside something you can't outrun
Don't touch temptation, what's held can't be undone
They'll promise not to bring you harm, as they pierce your palm
A delirium of its own making, there's no need to sound the alarm
A fear in them that you're faking, now which way to the crazy farm?

I made my peace with death
But mourn my own demise
Nothing but memories left
Forever fading, but the sun will rise ...

The mother tree

It ain't so much friction
More like a constant drag
But I ain't got the energy
To raise my white flag
No, I ain't got the energy
To raise my white flag ...

So I'll crawl upon this old cracked crane
With nothing to build to shelter from the rain
But what of him that carried the world alone
Just so others could catch a glimpse of the setting sun?
Flown past, like the bird with its song unknown
Free at last, yet never seeing you were the one

It ain't so much friction
More like a constant drag
But I ain't got the energy
To raise my white flag
No, I ain't got the energy
To raise my white flag ...

Like leaves whipped up into a frenzy
Circling but never stopping to ask where they're going
Never thinking to chastise the wind for blowing
So aimlessly beneath their mother tree
That's where you'll find me
Shoulders hunched, cajoled by the cold
Back from the wastelands, still so barren
Never finding my tongue to speak like Aaron
'Cos when you got nothing to say
Say nothing at all and be on your way

It ain't so much friction

More like a constant drag
But I ain't got the energy
To raise my white flag
No, I ain't got the energy
To raise my white flag ...

The door to nowhere

Presiding over the portico
naked men and women join hands
Never once kissing you know
for hands, they can say so much
Shining the soles of their dirty shoes for show
In twilight there's beauty, a certain lightness of touch
Like a giant using a dwarf's stature as his only crutch

Before offering to see the world clearer
See yourself for who you really are
Clear the mist from your mirror
Stop losing battles yet fought from afar
Then meet me at the border station
named for Peter the Great Tsar
Where flora from foreign lands stand in temple-like imitation
With a coffin-weight to take the strain of saluting the last train to where you
are ...

See the knight's horse pointed at the sea
It's time to toast our disavowal of Baltic tea
All that good work makes a fella thirsty!
As the professor questions the existence of equilateral triangles, another
warrior dies
He's examining the innards of books written on letter-free leaves, looking
you squarely in the eyes
"Destruction shows us what we're made of, the rest is what we believe!" he
sighs

Their faces like masks how they shine
In the clock tower's light, which is telling a useless time
Torsos twitted by their own shadows, so close they could be mine
Just in from the cold, the exiled executioner
He's on the look-out for better luck

To help the search, I give up my last few bucks
And his assistant, so reluctant
There's a hint of spirituality about him
Like the down-and-out merchants, men of great faith within
All believe they'll find the unbelieving, at the temple's gates without sin
As you and I walk through the door to nowhere, never speaking of where
we've been ...

Sweet Silvie

They can bury my body, but not my song
The melody plays on
The melody plays on ...
Laying the table with such pride
The sons of slaves all teary eyed
Tasting not the pain of their past
Exiled by the throngs
Though not one done wrong
But now I'm free at last!
At last we're free!
So dance with me
Sweet Silvie!

They're keen, but they'll never be seen
Showing any interest
Their hands are dirty, noses kept clean
The press'll tell you the rest
They avoid the blind
Like it's something contagious
And refuse the king's invitation
Afraid they'll say something outrageous!

We touched toes together in the rippling twilight
Holding hands handsomely in the misty moonlight
It must've looked like love at first sight
Maybe not upon closer inspection
But then you could never see much past your own reflection
And your mama's conventions
Could you sweet Silvie?

They can bury my body, but not my song
The melody plays on
The melody plays on ...

Laying the table with such pride
The sons of slaves all teary eyed
Tasting not the pain of their past
Exiled by the throngs
Though not one done wrong
But now I'm free at last!
At last we're free!
So dance with me
Sweet Silvie!

© Ed Fram 2017

Sunset's soldiers

Save your tears, heed my fears
Keep your flowers, the misused power
for sunset's soldiers
As a new empire rises on untested shoulders
The wise never knowing what it symbolises
To hold hope in their hands
But you're not the loving sort, Marie
So I'm collecting the pain you brought to me
'Cos everyone loves a good rainbow you see
Yeah, everyone loves a good rainbow but me

You can't sing a song
When the rhyme ain't right
You don't need to ask what's wrong
Honey, just hold me tight
But keep your flowers, the misused power
for sunset's soldiers
You'll need their favour when you're older
'Cos you're not the loving sort, Marie
But I'm collecting the pain you brought to me
'Cos everyone loves a good rainbow you see
Yeah, everyone loves a good rainbow but me

The furthest door needs no key
"So what made you leave?"
I asked out of curiosity
"We're all children of Eve"
You said so seriously
So keep your flowers, the misused power
for sunset's soldiers
We all need something to lean on when we lose composure
And you're not the loving sort, Marie
So I'm collecting the pain you brought to me

'Cos everyone loves a good rainbow you see
Yeah, everyone loves a good rainbow but me

Moon lake sonata

I must be outta my mind, I ain't the sensitive kind
But when they said chivalry was dead, I almost cried
Then you held the door for me with courtesy,
so I figure they must've lied
Now can I swim across your moon lake?
I'll do it in time to someone like Blake
For I know you admire him so!

But some day the tide too will tire
Of dousing liars in that great ol' fire
And this tale will pass down the ages
And the dust kept off its pages
So the warning can ring clean and clear
For those who greed for gifts and grub
The time is dawning, it's getting near ...

You say "I don't understand you!"
Honey, join the queue
You say "I don't need you!"
Well, that makes two

But go ahead, cling to the bandit
He's a seasoned professional
You can tell by his salt 'n' pepper hair
When he swears it's intentional
The only way to show you that he cares
But there's no sense questioning how you got here
The time is dawning now, darling it's getting near ...

You say "I don't understand you!"
Honey, join the queue
You say "I don't need you!"
Well, that makes two

I must be outta my mind, I ain't the sensitive kind
But when they said chivalry was dead, I almost cried
Then you held the door for me with courtesy,
so I figure they must've lied
Now can I swim across your moon lake?
I'll do it in time to someone like Blake
For I know you admire him so!

© Ed Fram 2016

Daybreak dreamer

My love with eyes that see, so fair and so far
Guide me through, wherever you now are
In the darkest night, babe be my wishing star
At the daybreak, be the strings to my guitar

See the gal with smokes and snakes
Don't you know she's holier than thou art?
Dreams as a rattle, gold dust in her shake
She'll defeat you, then tell you it's a start!
Darling with eyes that see, so fair and so far
Guide me through, wherever you now are

The shaman walks so low to the earth
Says there's less of a way to fall
But with the high net-worth
He's first in line to hear their call
Honey with eyes that see, so fair and so far
Guide me through, wherever you now are

"When you're wounded, I bleed"
The preacher crosses himself as he explains
"Whatever you want or need
I'll be here come shine or rain!"
My dear with eyes that see, so fair and so far
Guide me through, wherever you now are

My love with eyes that see, so fair and so far
Guide me through, wherever you now are
In the darkest night, babe be my wishing star
At the daybreak, be the strings to my guitar

© Ed Fram 2016

War and peace

She sang ole for her pay
I just sat facing this way and that
Whiling away another day
Scratching my head then my hat
I dunno if we choose God or God chooses us
All I know is all that glistens will soon be dust

She sang in Spanish
I danced in joy
Peace loves war
So said Tolstoy

You who delights in puns and paradox
The confounded better call the cops
With fears unfounded and unequalled
You of whom the followers speak so well
The famed interpreter of song and dream
This ain't no game, tell us what it all means

She sang in Spanish
I danced in joy
Peace loves war
So said Tolstoy

Writers and readers to a line or two, they're reduced at their death
A sound bite no more to a world hungry for noise is all they've now left
As the old battle rages, the machine men test their newest toys
And the bodies they float on red waves alongside blue buoys

She sang in Spanish
I danced in joy
Peace loves war
So said Tolstoy

Oh pearly rain, wash me clean
I'll be the shadow to your light
In time together we'll all be seen
As clearest day will be with night
In a land where golden hearts are crowns
And love is the only law
They'll be no more ups and downs
Only you forever more

She sang in Spanish
I danced in joy
Peace loves war
So said Tolstoy

A song to sadness

To a man, a monastery to catastrophe
A plan for treasure and trophies
Boldly taking their problems to the mountain
Seeking refunds for money in the fountain
While playing to absent audiences
Of senseless spirituality and coincidences
But who's prescribing the great sadness?

A cigar in one, a pen in the other
Light's out at end of this tunnel
Better go find me another
Though you never done me ill
Let me do more, let me do less
Open the door, I'll do the rest

Top button down by the convention of cool
As monkeys play beneath the ocean sky
Finding hopeless humanity a fool
For turning to zen when seeking why
Lost at sea in the ocean of randomness

Thank you for the sorrow
I had a lovely time
A fall will come tomorrow
But for now I'll enjoy the climb
"Me too baby, me too
Anything for you, anything for you"
Let me do more, let me do less
Open the door, I'll do the rest

© Ed Fram 2016

Forgive me, my friend

Forgive me my friend, to speak with a soul so meek
I know I did you wrong
Forgive me, I did you wrong
Gold I want naught, it's only your approval that I seek
Yet I'm cast away by the strong
Cast away by the strong!
But what nourishment is there in feeding from the weak?
So forgive me my friend, I know I did you wrong ...

It's better to die alone
Than to keep false company
So I'll lay down my bones
Among strangers at the cemetery

He that forceth through the marrow of time
Who knows what lies on the morrow for man
From whom darkness flees, brightly to shine
Knowing all in knowing only, God has a plan

Don't cry for me now
The river has flowed and gone
Don't ask about how
Just remember me in song

Forgive me my friend, to speak with a soul so meek
I know I did you wrong!
Forgive me, I did you wrong ...
Gold I want naught, it's only your approval that I seek
Still I'm cast away by the strong
Cast away by the strong!
Now what nourishment is there in feeding from the weak?
But you never forgave me, my friend

You wronged me at the end ...
You wronged me at the end ...

Sofa surfing

Sofa surfing to the waves beholden
The girl so fair, of locks a-golden
To her breast you were clinging
Eyes not open to attest the love she's bringing
Tears the life of the waters you're feeding
Cold to your cares as you lay there bleeding

Sofa surfing without the waves to carry ya
Never knowing what next they'll bring ya
A bucketful to hand, a cradle in the sand
To lay down your babe's head?
Even the shore ain't certain to find land
Pull down the curtain, this storm's well-fed

Sofa surfing, the waves ain't there to help ya
Not knowing where next they'll take ya
Drown'd to bed or washed-up instead
It could be either but it's never neither
For the girl we read, not a tear was shed
And tomorrow's sorrow will never revive her

Sofa surfing to the waves beholden
The girl so fair, of locks a-golden
To her breast you were clinging
Eyes not open to attest the love she's bringing
Tears the life of the waters you're feeding
Cold to your cares as you lay there bleeding

A hundred years hence

Now once upon a time, hear me out
Not like that, don't scream and shout
Long before the woods grew tall
And the first arrow flew in anger
In our hearts the wonder of it all
Brought silence to the slander
Some day darkness had to lose its way
Light up the path, it's judgement day!
'Twas all for you, so why do me wrong?
I love you true, it's why I write this song

When your better ain't the best
And you're tired of being put to the test
"Babe is this the sweetest you've ever heard?"
I ain't losing my mind, don't be absurd
But will they still like it a hundred years hence?
Tell me baby, quit sitting on the fence
You gotta give me some indication
Even Picasso's puzzles seek validation
But it's all for you, so why do me wrong?
I love you true, but I ain't that strong

Tearing past, a tidal force
Married at last, rain and divorce
Tell me straight, don't complain
Set a date for summer in Spain
Slow down but don't be late
Gold's never worth its own weight
See the hot dollars, they're quickly drying
And the merchants, they'll be crying!

But it's all for you, now why do me wrong?
I love you true, it's why I wrote this song

Our place

Grab the tab double-quick
Too much of nothing can make a man sick
Turn out the lights so I can see you good
Free me like you said you would
And take me to where they adorn
Torn clothes like they've never been worn

Where it's read before it's written
Where it's felt from well within
Where my feet may stumble
Where my hands still tremble
At the hint of your blue-green glint

In that place
there's nothing to do but love
So I'll set my prayers free
on the wings of a dove
And turn to see my shadow smile
Around here, babe, no man's an isle

Beneath your streets in rows
all quaint and cobbled
Egos are inflated head to toe
after the stake's been doubled
So take me to where they scorn
the loudest and latest yet born

Where it's read before it's written
Where it's felt from well within
Where my feet may stumble
Where my hands still tremble
At the hint of your blue-green glint

In that place
there's nothing to do but love
So I'll set my prayers free
on the wings of a dove
And turn to see my shadow smile
Around here, babe, no man's an isle

© Ed Fram 2016

Becoming

I ain't for you to borrow
I ain't for you to buy
I'm just gonna sit here and sigh
Thinking of becoming
The top drawer
It don't always hold the best stuff
Go on! Take the smooth with the rough
It's tough, floating beneath the waves
At your own homecoming

Persecution his birthright, destitution a dying sight
In a land measuring mediocrity by the bucket load
While Eternity comes on the head of a pin
And with his swords crossed, the crusader showed
Fighting for a God he scarcely believes in

Now the kids, they're wanting change
But still finding Marx quite revolting
With nothing to protest, it feels strange
Lessons spotting communists feel insulting
Another peace demo, more anti-war ammo
To fire at the coolest kid I know
A wise head on shoulders so young
But time's moved me on
To thinking of becoming

I'll set myself apart, out on the fringes
You can't close a door without hinges
Do you know why you do what you do?
Share your secret and I'll share mine too
See the show monkey's tired of the circus
He's in the audience, he don't dig the fuss
And the mockingbird's humming

Thinking it's arrived
But I'm busy becoming
And learning to survive

Cut the cable if you're able
For the headliner with the sellout slap
"No good can come of this
Be a nice chap and boo, don't clap"
We'll beat them at their own game
In the rain, you'd better trade tricks
It's coming on fast and thick
A sceptic floating beneath the waves
At your own homecoming

And each man has his own path
To glory or tears in the bath
But we all just wanna go home
The gardens I'm shown, I've outgrown
Hand me the phone, so I can moan
At the faceless tone I've disowned
And as everyone walks out
"I'm still here!" you'll shout
Staying crazy to the end
"But baby I'm your friend"
If so, tear down the clocks
Making forever sound
In a studio that time forgot
Honey, I'm busy becoming

If I wrote then

If I wrote then
I'd have told
Of all the little things
That mean so much
I'd wind back the spool's threads
To undo the touch
And stand on what's said
Amid the mutiny of the madhouse
Where the music stops
And the little boy dances

But there's no use trying
Like an artist slowly dying
In a world denying
All knowledge of colour
So we learn to stand naked
Without seeking cover
Believing together we'll make it

If I wrote then
I'd have told
Of how the sun set
All cold
Before we met
I'd have told
Of streams we never crossed
Of boat rides and when you got lost
With love untasted

But there's no use trying
Like an artist slowly dying
In a world denying
All knowledge of colour

So we learn to stand naked
Without seeking cover
Believing together we'll make it

If I wrote then
I'd have told
Of empty rounds like cockroaches
All around
As suddenly death approaches
Without a sound
Its hungry eyes wandering
To where the music stops
And the little boy dances

But there's no use trying
Like an artist slowly dying
In a world denying
All knowledge of colour
So we learn to stand naked
Without seeking cover
Believing together we'll make it

It's not love yet

All the people rushing around
Must be a war on I said
But I ain't heard a sound
Maybe I'll end up dead
That's when I noticed you
Confidently donning a bright pink hat
You caught mind before my eye
Seemed too pretty to be travelling like that
And you left me questioning why ...

You say I got a funny way of telling the same old tales
Feeding you with words that'll never go stale
Like how the best always know how to fail
But I'm still looking for answers to show me you care
No girl, there's no need to fret
Ain't reason to worry 'bout what you'll wear
It's not love yet
But it's getting there

Feed the flower
The seed is sown
It's not about your power
Only everything you own
The date is set
No more a pair
It's not love yet
But we're getting there

I been an actor, but never told a lie
Yet even the comic must sometimes cry
And come judgement day
We'll all be sent on our way
Keeping only what matters, rest in tatters

Remembering reckless chatter leads to regret
All the while, I'm a captive to your free flowing hair
It's not love yet
But we're nearly there

Honey, hold your fire
Recharge the armory
I ain't saying you're a liar
You're misunderstanding me
Wait for everything to transpire
Before sending in the cavalry
There's no more land to get
Beyond where you stare
It's not love yet
But we're almost there

The teacher, he's granting the final grade
Valuing the riches they think they made
Testing their metal, hammering and heating
A scene so surreal it's worth repeating
Just to be sure all accounts are settled
He gives another bang to their metal
As the proud, in they come tip-toeing
Unsure how to act around the mercy he's showing
Like people who've only just met
Knowing taking sides in love will leave them square
It's not love yet
But we're nearly there

Those words, payment they don't seek any
Their followers are so few
Their readers, they are many
But what do they see looking up at you?
The creep of urban villages at your doorstep
Out of keep with cane and tail tours

By the young and helpless who wept
With no vision for their futures
Seeing in the new year regardless
In their bright pink hats I guess ...

You ain't seen nothing yet

Painted women with the night prince
Courted then but never since
Hand it over and wish you'd not met
A blindfold for Jez
Resonating with your wrinkles of regret
And her look that says
You ain't seen nothing yet

A square stare and a freedom flare
Captain Hook riding on a legless chair
Chocking amid smoking sailors
You're enjoying it still
Who needs books, watch the trailer
And pop another pill
With the promise never to fail her

The chorus masters are well-versed
You never had the chance to rehearse
I know it ain't easy my friend
Catching riddles at half mast
Empty hands with good wishes to send
But the time is now, better act fast
So take what's been penned

Memorise a mosaic of feather-faced femmes
But don't touch what's madam's
Stay right there, you aren't to know
How the spineless rest
With skinned origins like the snow
Thinking their way is best
Or so the story goes

Painted women with the night prince

Courted then but never since
Hand it over and wish you'd not met
A blindfold for Jez
Resonating with your wrinkles of regret
And her look that says
You ain't seen nothing yet

© Ed Fram 2016

Forever bells

Shirley now moonlit in silence
Her eyes, you've never seen them
And she'll overpower your defiance
Till there's nothing left to condemn

Forever bells haven't been rung
But we know we'll never part
I know you like my native tongue
You speak to me from the heart

Shirley now lays so soft
A look all warm and tender
My hands, they'll float aloft
As to her will, I surrender

Our forever bells ring
We'll never be apart
Let me hear you sing
Singing from the heart

But who you gonna blame
If the gate ain't pearly?
Claim and counterclaim
Won't you give up Shirley?

Our forever bells rung
But when we did part
I went for young
She went for smart

Shirley now moonlit in silence
Her eyes, you've never seen them

And she'll overpower your defiance
Till there's nothing left to condemn

© Ed Fram 2016

Cold hearts

Ain't no need to name those to blame
They know who they are
Ain't no need to name those to blame
They know who they are
So go on inviting cold hearts to the fire
There's reaping to do, better fetch me a rake
But the more I give, the more that they take
Grab a pen, this time won't come again
Like a king in his own way, back to a pawn the next day

Ain't it a shame you never came
You know who you are
Ain't it a shame you never came
You know who you are
So gather up cold hearts for the fire
The more I understand, the less I really know
The more I know, the less I really understand
Now who's gonna show me the way to go?
Like long ago. O! how we figured and planned

Ain't that just like me, you now claim
But I don't know who you are
Ain't that just like me, you now claim
But I don't know who you are
So keep collecting cold hearts for the fire
See our love for each other
It could only grow from our love for another
Like ash on a no smoking sign
If you wanna complain, wait in line

Ain't no need to name those to blame
They know who they are
Ain't no need to name those to blame

They know who they are
So go on inviting cold hearts to the fire
You can be first back or the last to leave
Whatever you now believe
But when you ain't got the key for the gate
Your melting heart will suffer its fate ...

Je t'aime

Winds blow on by
The sands ain't shifting
Winds blow on by
The sands ain't shifting
'Neath crates of cares
They'll need heavy lifting

Words too hard to say
I already spoke them
Words too hard to say
I already spoke them
Don't leave me babe
Je t'aime, je t'aime, je t'aime

When you're tired of sleep
With no one else to turn to
When you're tired of sleep
With no one else to turn to
Nothing can ever be known
If we only listen to speak

The fool with no limit to his talent
He'll keep on loving you
The fool with no limit to his talent
He'll keep on loving you
As sure as the sun
But he can't tell you what it meant

The death arrows fly
Finger tight on the trigger
The death arrows fly
Finger tight on the trigger
Deaf to peace drums

Deaf past babies that cry

Now why point the finger
At the point of a gun?
Now why point the finger
At the point of a gun?
The death arrows fly
They don't know to linger

It meant nothing then
Even less to me now
It meant nothing then
Even less to me now
Someday deadwood will be coal
For pencil or pen
And from the heart you stole
Je t'aime, je t'aime, je t'aime

Faye's fable

Watching people, people watching
I saw some Moscow punks
They like freedom and think the rest is junk
Watching people, people watching
I called out to those that go back
To shadows in reverse from chemical flashbacks
Past the hackers with nothing left to hack

The hour to take your hand
It has come and gone
Charcoal cares in the sand
where the moon once shone
Their Sumerian silk, your gilded guilt
Can you wish it all away?
Oh tell me true, fair lady Faye
How long will they make you stay?

Watching people, people watching
I saw stalkers picnic by the roadside
With reality their new play thing
"Anything can be anything
But nothing can't be nothing" they all sing
As fountains of red continue to pour
For those that marched on before
To the beat of a counter culture you can count on but can't defeat
So sing to the tune of the bloody peace they'll secure

The town on the hill
That you promised to protect
Where the people love you still
But you'd rather forget
Their Sumerian silk, your gilded guilt
Can you wash your hands of it?

Will you let these rose guns wilt?
Oh fair lady Faye, look at what we've built

Watching people, people watching
I met a girl who seeks only to change the world
I told her what you're looking for is in the mirror
Not in the way your hair is curled
She said the edge of humanity is getting nearer
It's clear we're on the brink
So I turned away from her, I had no idea what to think

A new moon lighting up the lake
Your vision of finery and furs
There's not a promise left to break
But I can't tell you if it's hers
Their Sumerian silk, your gilded guilt
Is your chalice filled to the hilt?
Oh fair lady Faye, will your steeple stand on silt?
Their Sumerian silk, your gilded guilt
Can you wash your hands of it?
Will you let these rose guns wilt?
Oh fair lady Faye, look at what we've built ...

© Ed Fram 2016

Anthem of Anthemusa

The hair, pure water falling
Into the fairest hand I've known
If I could make a drawing
Or maybe a tapestry I had sewn
To drink from at the dawning
To drink from you alone ...

You won my chapeau
Then sent me on my way
Another jolly nice fellow
Least that's what I heard you say

You spared my soul
Whatever's left of it
My love you stole
Then claimed it counterfeit

Now why do you speak like that?
There's nothing special here to grasp
You better give me back my hat
And I'll hand you back your mask

The hair, pure water falling
Into the fairest hand I've known
If I could make a drawing
Or maybe a tapestry I had sewn
To drink from at the dawning
To drink from you alone ...

© Ed Fram 2016

For whom

For whom
does the blossom bloom?
If not for you,
then show me for who

Why does the river run
to where others won't walk?
Who'd give up their son
for those who can only balk?

A grain of truth washes up
on every shore
Your smile passing down
into folklore

Who could smooth the seas
with their calming kiss?
Death's a matter of degrees
from the serpent's hiss

That spring, like a new babe's breath
Lifted us up, then we up and left
With faces cloaked in wicked wonder
At his scarlet robes ripped asunder

Forever is a day
I've not yet tasted
The moments fade away
But never wasted

© Ed Fram 2016

A dying art

The swine and the swindler, they take from one trough
The silent foot of death is behind you from the off
But a holier outlaw than he, I've never seen
A medicine man and the orphan's friend he's been
Beauty draws the eye
Truth colours the soul
This crazy life's a lie
Loveless loving takes its toll

The best artists steal
But crime is a dying art
I can't promise you a deal
Of heavy purse and light heart

So tread softly through
Where the smell of violence lays
You'll be gone a week or two
No word how much it pays
But it's sure to be a sum enough
For a vice or two children
Selling the fruits of toil for scruff
Taking your sword to the pen
Two houses but no home's a bluff
For learning to breathe again

The best artists steal
But crime is a dying art
I can't promise you a deal
Of heavy purse and light heart

Now each stone has a silent story
While the home tells a tall tale
But never replace his glory

Lest you hear the walls wail
For death's never far from everyday life
And always on your tail
Beauty draws the eye
Truth colours the soul
This crazy life's a lie
Loveless loving takes its toll

The best artists steal
But crime is a dying art
I can't promise you a deal
Of heavy purse and light heart

© Ed Fram 2016

Picture perfect

Take me laughing, take me crying
They say your words oughta stop me dying
But I gotta stop living so you can live in me
That don't sound like any way to be free
So I guess I'll keep listening to the voices
Of this generation, silenced by the next
Gotta make some hard, hard choices
The world expects

The random rambler knows the way to go
Been places no right-minded body can know
Follow him gladly, follow him proud
Just don't talk too much or too loud
If it ain't worth saying in your head
Better put that slumberin' scrawl to bed
See how for the camera, one smiles and one salutes
Both knowin' it's a timeless shoot ...
Both knowin' it's a timeless shoot ...

Captured in the cold, frozen frame
This image can't be sold, not for fortune or fame
To the storytellers and men with pens
And all the victors, who history defends
Make way for the time is drawin' near
The sands have passed back to the sea
Now I see it all, it's clear to me
Blessed saviour come to live in me ...
Blessed saviour come to live in me ...

Why?

Now the lady with the line drawings
she's in a room of blue velvet
Where cherubs crack whips and teeth a-gnawing
At the serpent, who has nothing left to covet
And we'll die trying
though we ain't dying to try
We'll ask how
though we're really wondering why

But my tears do not move you
My sorrow even less
Tell me where you're going to
Even the priest must some day confess
And you'll die trying
though you ain't dying to try
You'll ask me how
though you're really wondering why

Don't deny me this deathly dance, right to the floor
Though the swagger is gone, there's a sway to display
A clipped gladioli from the one I adore
Like you always say, I must have my way
And so, I'll die trying
though I ain't dying to try
I'll ask how
though I'm left wondering why

Rose

When nearly ain't nearly enough
When your dear ain't dear to you
It's tough
Give me a week without bread and not a minute without her breath
Rip up the pictures and cross out the day when happiness left
They say success follows failure
They say failure follows success
I'll keep following you, oh saviour
The only way I'll pass this test

Some love too little, others love too much or many
How can two from the same cup drink any?
Like Monica and Maeve and his morbid muse
Hour after hour with attic scribbles to amuse
Always in the moment
But I'll pace around the past
It's pretty here
Black and white simplicity
No taboo of authenticity
Yes, it was once pretty here

But now even hush money talks
From the same trunk spring the green and the rotten
Speaking of some deeper love
Long after the roots have been forgotten
A witness to wisdom weighing more than gold
They say success follows failure
They say failure follows success
I'll keep following you, oh saviour
The only way I'll pass this test

With poems and pints we'll put the world right
Even the high commissioner's never felt so low

No use hiding in plain sight
with hopes hanging by a thread
Begging and borrowing so
thoughts of giving in filling you with dread
No this slate ain't for cleaning
No use fearing fate, searching, scheming or California dreaming
She's here now, my Rose
with nothing to prove
She ain't playing at poetry over pints and prose
Her smile too mysterious for the Louvre
Ah! Rose's smile...

They say too much luck will kill you
That's why I'm still around
Trying to say something old in a new way and make it seem profound
But why do I feel so lonely, when you're here to stay?
Can we really play it the same way
with a better outcome like you say?
There ain't no time for tears
When telling time from a crooked clock
The farmers don't know how to measure the cow, as sunset nears
Now pink pills for the pale and poor, while the shepherds count their flock
As we think of what life has in store
They say success follows failure
They say failure follows success
I'll keep following you, oh saviour
The only way I'll pass this test

Ah! To think of what life has in store, with its fickle fate
You came into it too early and left your return so very late
But how could I hit the target, when I couldn't see what I was aiming for?
How could I move forward, when my dreams were trapped behind your
door?
That door for dreaming came and went, as a night's sleep
So let's hold this door of memory ajar

For the thorn was always close and the rose so very far
As we dream of red mansions under the same star ...

Hold me close

Just sitting here in the frozen traffic
Waiting to be shown the way
Empty thinking, with no weapon to attack it
"I'm only asking to be asked!" you say
"But where's the game changer when you need it?
Or will I always just have to pay?
Hold me close
Tell me it'll be ok."

You've got no answers, but you need my questions
To feed the idea machines
It's filled with Valentine rejections
The have-nots and might-have-beens
The river, it carries many reflections
With its fill of past faces and olden scenes
And the course, it forever changes
But I know you'd never lead me astray
Just hold me close
Tell me it'll be ok

Thirteen white horses on the horizon
Just the way it goes sometimes
It's hard luck I only wanted a dozen
You can change their thoughts but not their minds
And the crew, they come dressed in crimson
Juggling fear and love with their unearned finds
"At stately homes they'll impress you, my son
But not forever, not till the end of times."
"Hear me father, show me the way
Hold me close
Tell me it'll be ok."

© Ed Fram 2016

Oh gentle one

He don't care for fashion
He's come to see your soul
To reclaim the rejected ration
And all the things you stole

So come softly, oh gentle one
Come near enough to touch
Come soon before it's all gone
More can never be too much

Love's ladder is leaning against
a wall of uncertain foundation
Marble waters across false dawns
are telling of hell's own damnation

So come softly, oh gentle one
Come near enough to touch
Come soon before it's all gone
More can never be too much

Now, be still for the winds to cease
Though the leaves rustle round
My heart was never yours to release
I was never lost to be found

So come softly, oh gentle one
Come near enough to touch
Come soon before it's all gone
More can never be too much

Dancing on the ceiling

I see the words so clearly
High up on the wall
"To the one I hold so dearly"
They're warning of a fall
I've received them sincerely
But who else could I call?

The winner's taken it all
Ain't nothing in my bag
Not walking quite so tall
Now throw me another rag
To tease and enthrall
Though never to brag

The money's all dried up
But hope's still flowin'
Words spoken in spite to the discontent
Greeted with love by the establishment
But why does sleep come so easy
When you don't need the rest?
Why's everything you've always wanted
blown away before the test?

You turn this way, I'll turn that
Quickly now, this ain't no time to chat
From the outset, we were doomed
Meeting on a cloudy sorta afternoon
When we weren't even close
That's when you wanted me most
But hope's left the building
So must I, farewell, adios

Sometimes I get this feeling

The writing ain't on the wall
It's dancing on the ceiling
Above where you fall
And time, it ain't for healing
Passing till I don't know you at all

At sixes and sevens

Who said what first, to whom and why
We're at sixes and sevens, that I can't deny
You say you still care, that much I got
But you were never one to nurture and replenish
"Take this and leave, enough now that's your lot!"
Like a wave come to wash away an unwelcome wish
"Accept me as I am", so solemnly you declare
But from the fruits of their labouring hands you ate
Day after day, never leaving a morsel to share
Not a crumb until it was too late

"I knew what I wanted then
I couldn't tell you that now
Nothing turns out as planned
And the planned turns in to nothing
But when I say I'll meet all your demands
You say that I'm only bluffing

The river and the sea
They seem strange bedfellows to me
One be near, one still so far
One flows, as the other roars
Yet one, and at once, they are
Beneath the light, oh how it soars!
But could a star shine so bright
If not surrounded by the dark?
How could I know wrong from right
If I'd never strayed wide of the mark?"

© Ed Fram 2015

Home again

In the dawning half-light
Of our congested sprawl
Glimpse the crow mid-flight
And see me giving it my all

I ain't got a penny
But you make me feel like a millionaire
Fame - I ain't got any
But wherever we go people stop and stare

When the door slams
Windows open silently
She's another man's
She whispers to me softly

I ain't got a penny
But you make me feel like a millionaire
Fame - I ain't got any
But wherever we go people stop and stare

A sunset so crisp and clean
A child's smile so pure
No greater joy has there been
You coming back to me once more

Kiss me

Kiss me to carnage.
I'll love you to submission.
Nothing's changed since the Stone Age.
I'm a man on a mission ...

Close among the fiefdoms of the faithless.
They can only let you down!
Still following the paces of the placeless,
like tumbleweed across their torched towns.
For you, my dear, there's no home to be found.
There's no home to be found ...

They pass on by, he that rocks for socks,
to cover his sore soles.
But their pain will outlast this hidden healing.
Their new money's getting old pretty fast.
The false gods they've bankrolled won't last, soon they'll be squealing!
Scrambling to swap keys for locks on their past.
But now's too late for their grieving.
It's too late for their grieving ...

You never cared for this lifeless living.
Stuck between the bridges where you once bathed so free.
Snarling "darling won't you come back to me!"
Now your mind's in the lost and found.
But I never gave up wanting you around.
No, I never gave up wanting you around ...

Kiss me to carnage.
I'll love you to submission.
Beyond our golden age,
on the road to perdition ...

Rivers of gold

All together, with pointed purpose we'll rise
The little boy looks wilder as he dies
Once we swam rivers
We swam rivers of gold
Now the waters are cold, so very cold!

With earthly poets our skies unfold
'Neath starry blankets our glory foretold
Of how we swam rivers
We swam rivers of gold
Now the waters are cold, so very cold!

All that stands between wolf and dog
A few green leaves and the clearing fog
Where once we swam rivers
We swam rivers of gold
Now the waters are cold, so very cold!

© Ed Fram 2017

To becoming

The Romans reclining over ruins
That must be believed to be seen
With their furs of future fury
Long since abandoned
To the reckless twists of time
To discourse and digressions too numerous to name
They went, they came
In their place Nirvanic confusion
But could we have fallen this far without first raising our heads
Past parapets so everlastingly ephemeral?
To glance just beyond our own darkest delusion
To know what became of them
To know what became of us
As the Romans recline over ruins ...

© Ed Fram 2017

Chasing dreams

The craziest thing I ever seen
You wouldn't believe it
Not even in a dream

The passive punching thin air
The rich, they live in Bel Air
The highway's full of lowlifes
Society's fabric ain't formed
without a knife
Scarlet scandals, political reform
Socks and sandals in a storm
Light the candle, a new norm
Progress is overrated

The craziest thing I ever seen
You wouldn't believe it
Not even in a dream

© Ed Fram 2017

Tears in my tequila

Tears in my tequila
Rain taps at your door
The sun's got the idea
It ain't welcome no more

Our dreams in the closet
Under lock and key
With no gold to deposit
Baby it's just you and me

No more rules for breaking
All's put to the test
This fool's heart ain't for taking
He left it out West

Pictures speak many words
That cannot be said
The most beautiful thing I never heard
You kept to yourself instead

Tears in my tequila
Rain taps at your door
The sun's got the idea
It ain't welcome no more

© Ed Fram 2017

You ain't back yet

I know this ain't my place no more, but there was nowhere else to go
As ancient voices whisper of all the people I used to know
And her smile, the first place I ever called home
Our home, the first place I ever really smiled

But tell me, who ever painted his house in misery
Only to burn the bristles in regret?
I've waited a long while, but you ain't back yet, you ain't back yet ...

Even the beautiful gotta win ugly sometimes
It means whatever you want, when you read between the lines
Look up from time to time, you never know what you might find
I'd hand you a clue, if only I knew your mind

But tell me, who ever painted his house in misery
Only to burn the bristles in regret?
I've waited a long while, but you ain't back yet, you ain't back yet ...

When the only thing worth seeing is hidden to your eyes
When the only thing worth feeling turns out to be lies
Like the haunted hunter, battered bear coat by his side
Ensnared by his own trap, with no place left to hide

But tell me, who ever painted his house in misery
Only to burn the bristles in regret?
I've waited a long while, but you ain't back yet, you ain't back yet ...

The snowman

Until you escape time, you'll never really be free
When you feel no love, you'll know what it's like to be me
"Come in from there, you must be so cold" they'll say
"I was formed from frozen sky, leave me be if you may"
Leave me be in the cold all day ...
Leave me be in the cold all day ...

We can't unwind the winds of change
I'm younger than yesterday itself
I noticed you noticing me, so strange
But your heart seemed some place else
"Baby show me that you care
And I'll show you all my loving"
"Oh come on, that's hardly fair
First show me that lost loving
Then I'll show you how much I care"

The future's a debt we can't ever cover
Ask the rarely repentant, frequently faithless lover
Or the prince who hates what decorum dictates
Crying "our pain's the same, we're just suffering from different fates!"
"Now climb off your high horse and chant your highness, your chariot
awaits!"

You once said, we can't dance without stepping on toes
It's just the way it goes
And to serve reclining Romans, some must stay upright at all times
Go ask the poet, who no longer cares if it rhymes
As for me, no longer dare I dream
Life's already fanciful in the extreme

Yet soon all may be as it seems
Yes, I read it in some magazine
Over the prince's shoulder
Take your new coat, you'll need it when it's older
And it's raining in the dry house ...

There's no sense in chasing the sun, while looking out for rain
Spending Sundays spying on love, you never know what it's hiding again
But you didn't care enough to deny me, all I might ask
And there's enough crying rain to fill another flask
Honey, pull down that mask
Reveal the girl without a face
Long ago you took my heart
And left me without a place

When you got nothing left to believe in
You better start praying boy
When you can't even buy a win
You'll remember the world once was your toy
Like the pauper in love, with no way to show it
They'll call you "lost property" or at least missing in transit
As the snowman points his cigar at the sky, he's back
With poison plumes, the rain turns black
The sole smoker in the Siberian snow
Ask politely and he'll point the way to go
Perilously peering at the cliff edge you're nearing, at the dawning of new day
Past a statue so still, she's seen it all before, silently guiding you along the
way
To where the crazy have wild thoughts for company, you'll point your boat
Wearing the snowman's coat, with all his ideas to promote
For he's left them in your suitcase ...

Until you escape time, you'll never really be free
When you feel no love, you'll know what it's like to be me
"Come in from there, you must be so cold" they'll say
"I was formed from frozen sky, leave me be if you may"
Leave me be in the cold all day ...
Leave me be in the cold all day ...

4355

I kissed you like it was the first time
You kissed me like it was the last
I held you like you were still mine
You let me drift into your past

The more you're given
The more they'll expect to get
They say you're forgiven
But I ain't felt it yet

Pity you looking all gloom and glum
Just like a pirate all out of rum
But it ain't like it's your life in his hands
He ain't after the earth, just your land
For what it's worth, I'd do as he demands

The regal and the revolutionary
Arm in arm how they strode
"Confusion needn't be scary!"
Says the maid speaking in code
"Join us, we're tearing up this road!"

"Four three five five, boy look alive!
I'll give your cage a rattle, be sure not to skive!"
But the chief, he'll sell you smokes a nickel
As long as you give his ego a tickle
And a tipple for strength to blow on his whistle

The more you're given
The more they'll expect to get
They say you're forgiven
But I ain't felt it yet

I kissed you like it was the first time
You kissed me like it was the last
I held you like you were still mine
You let me drift into your past

© Ed Fram 2017

The philosopher's musings

China's Sherlock is here to take stock
Of what the intelligence units left behind
While a parrot atop the grandfather clock
Tells you the imperial sands have shifted
But what can you say
When your luck is down and your time is up?
When the riches they pay
Are beyond compare, it's time to drink up!

Silver frames and golden shades
And all the beauty man's made
Are real and wholly unbecoming
While from the walls, jewels and serpents hang free
But what can you say
When your luck is down and your time is up?
When the riches they pay
Are beyond compare, it's time to drink up!

The mutinous show mercy
To the rapacious and ravenous
Who are let loose on their bounty
While discord dances to the philosopher's musings
But what can you say
When your luck is down and your time is up?
When the riches they pay
Are beyond compare, it's time to drink up!

With a bag of rags on my back,
And a suitcase full of dreams
I'll make my way home
I'll make my way home …
For what can you say
When your luck is down and your time is up?

When the riches they pay
Are beyond compare, it's time to drink up!

© Ed Fram 2015

A prayer tonight

I'll raise a remembrance stone to the sky
To the sky, to know why
Though it can never reach that high, my dear
No, it can never reach that high …

Faded and free, as though but a dream
There, I could tell you how I really feel
Without all the panic, infinite time to steal
Faded and free, 'twas but a dream
Who will now show the way?
The ghost hears, though deaf to all I pray

I'll raise a remembrance stone to the sky
To the sky, to know why
Ah! It can never reach that high, my love
No, it can never reach that high …

So with the men at work, I'll satisfy myself
Lugging, chugging and chinking
Amidst their slander and all-night drinking
With the men at work, I'll lose myself
The men are at work, machinery's at play
Destined to divide, for now united we'll stay

I'll raise a remembrance stone to the sky
To the sky, to know why
Though it can never reach that high, my dear
No, it can never reach that high …

Like the paschalia full of pain but promise
Alone you flourished and floundered there
While for the sea of red, the people came to stare
To think of the great sacrifice and not the avarice

Of the ones that sent them there
Of the ones that sent them there

I'll raise a remembrance stone to the sky
To the sky, to know why
Ah! It can never reach that high, my love
No, it can never reach that high ...

Meant to be

Power passes
The baton slips
Time ceases
The race flips
The first is last
The last, first
The silence is deathly
Static wheels on a hearse
The mourners gather, some barely survive
Out of misery, others thrive
But only the dead know what it means to be alive
Yes, only the dead know what it means to be alive …

© Ed Fram 2015

The artist

Every love song that was ever written
Ain't enough
When with the wrong man you're smitten
His affection, it's only free if you pay double you see
Now come to me, to give to each other unconditionally
Though we're late to the game
The rules never change
Shoot straight without aim
Keep your nose clean
Ignore the referee's screams
And we'll do just fine
Yes we'll do just fine

You don't need a weather man to believe in
To know, when it rains it ain't poured out even
Empty hands are all you're seeing
While he takes three cups full just for being
But all the money can't afford him life everlasting
That only comes through true love, prayer and fasting
So he'll be shamed like a judge caught on the wrong side of his own law
Then again what do I know, no mind for a living, 'stead I use my paw
But say you'll be mine
And we'll do just fine
Yes we'll do just fine

They'll all wonder, just how did he do it
From where did the ideas come?
If you just can't see it
Better line up, go tap on my drum
For the artist, he paints blind
And the colours follow behind
Yes the artist, he paints blind
And the colours follow behind

They'll ask about our happiness
But we know they really couldn't care less
Yes, they'll ask about our happiness
But we know they really couldn't care less
Say how you feel and spare us the rest!
Say how you feel, don't be wasting our time
For we're doing just fine
Yes we're doing just fine

The sea of reeds

So long honey babe, take care leaving town
They say all good things come to an end
But the bad's gotta end too some time
Lighten up, your gravity's dragging me down
It ain't that I had no more lovin' to send
But pay me no mind babe, I'll be doing fine
For there's a time to live
And a time to kill
A time to laugh
And a time to cry
A time to miss you
And a time to ask why

How long can we live on past glories?
The end's known before hearing the full story
Where were you when the sea of reeds was parted?
The end is well known, though not how it started
But pay me no mind babe, I'll be doing fine
For there's a time to live
And a time to kill
A time to laugh
And a time to cry
A time to miss you
And a time to ask why

Some eat away the sadness
Others let sadness eat away at them
Some see flowers of happiness
Others only the lone stem
But pay me no mind babe, I'll be doing fine
For there's a time to live
And a time to kill
A time to laugh

And a time to cry
A time to miss you
And a time to ask why

Perfectly imperfect

If I had but to write, telling of that which is perfectly imperfect
Where truth and lies can be the same, in substance and effect
Where the faithless and the faithful can never again reconnect
Where all around is made to be perfectly imperfect
Would you placate me with platitudes or say it wasn't worth it?
For who but the counting crow knows each wave of the sky's seas?
Howbeit he resteth on scrawny shoulders, when you're down on your
knees!
To sit and gaze admiringly at forgotten faces, from times not yet passed
To be there at her final breath, when angels and their agents are unmasked
So I'll keep on telling all, of that which is perfectly imperfect
Where truth and lies can be the same, in substance and effect
Where the faithless and the faithful can never again reconnect
Where all around is made to be perfectly imperfect

© Ed Fram 2015

Covered in blue

It's said death awaits all, yet it waits for no man
How will you get there, with a map but no plan?

It was a tidy crime, the setting was sublime
As I held you outside the law one last time
But I can't be gripping with open hands
and this closed heart
I can't hold back the desert sands
after our false start
So leave me here, take your troubles too
If you don't mean it, why ask what I'll do?
And the painter, he knows every hue
Though everything's now covered in blue ...

The river runs where we've walked before
To follow no one, still forever led to shore
We're free to chose, so long as we call it right
We're led to darkness, only then to see the light
You always held the key, though the door remains hidden
The truth is, I'm just grateful for what we weren't given
For the painter, he knows every hue
Yet everything's still covered in blue ...

It's official, though it ain't been declared
You could tell by the name he beared
Sent to solemnly guard what's yet to be granted
Sent to preside over prayers and all they chanted
To send them back from whence they came
With their ideals, the land just ain't the same
And for the painter who knows every hue
Everything's still covered in blue ...

Just as death awaits all, yet it waits for no man
How will you get there, with a map but no plan?

Forefathers and more

Pour forth your worldly waters
Gently stroke the stones of the shore
You built your wall to resist the mortars
Of enemies to forefathers and more ...

But how long will it weather the waves
To speak to all the stories of the brave?
To stand tall amidst the ruins 'neath the island of your heart
To see the anguish of loves left unloved,
though never apart
To signal of lands never journeyed, now gone too long
To remind you and I of what we knew all along ...

Pour forth your worldly waters
Gently stroke the stones of the shore
You built your wall to resist the mortars
Of enemies to forefathers and more ...

Treachery is only clear to the treacherous
There's no place 'round here to call a home
But adventure will no more left to the adventurous
I knew that when you came to the feast all alone
Yet see how the temple still stands tall and dedicated
To a memory born of spirit, once lived never eradicated

So pour forth your worldly waters
Gently stroke the stones of the shore
You built your wall to resist the mortars
Of enemies to forefathers and more ...

© Ed Fram 2015